The Library of the Thirteen Colonies and the Lost Colony™

The Colony of Maryland

Brooke Coleman

The Rosen Publishing Group's
PowerKids Press™
New York

To Both My Daniels

Published in 2000 by The Rosen Publishing Group, Inc.
29 East 21st Street, New York, NY 10010

Photo Credits: p. 1 © Archive Photos; pp. 4, 8, 11, 16, 20 © Corbis-Bettman; pp. 7, 12, 15, 19 © SuperStock; p. 22 © Janet W. Connor/Historic St. Mary's City

First Edition

Book Design: Andrea Levy

Coleman, Brooke
      Maryland / by Brooke Coleman.
          p.   cm. — (The library of the thirteen colonies and the Lost Colony series)
      Includes index.
      Summary: An introduction to the early days of the settlement of Maryland, describing the daily life and economy of the colony and its religious tolerance.
      ISBN 0-8239-5483-8
      1. Maryland—History—Colonial period, ca. 1660–1775—Juvenile literature. [1. Maryland—History—Colonial period, ca. 1660–1775.] I. Title. II.
      Series.
      F184 .C65 1999
      975.2'02—dc21

                                                                                                        98-32364
                                                                                                            CIP
                                                                                                            AC

Manufactured in the United States of America

Contents

A Charter for the Calverts

In England in the 1600s and 1700s, people of different religions did not get along. The King said that everyone had to be **Protestant**. **Catholics** could be jailed or even killed for their religion. A rich Englishman named Sir George Calvert wanted to create a place where Catholics could be free to live without anyone bothering them. Other Europeans looking for a new life had settled in America. Calvert decided this is where he would go too. In 1632, King Charles I of England gave the Calvert family a **charter** to start a **colony** north of Colonia Virginia. The Calverts had to use their own money to start the colony, but they got to make all the laws. The colony was to be called Maryland after King Charles's wife, Henrietta Maria.

◄ *George Calvert hoped that people of different religions could live together peacefully.*

5

Maryland Is Born

George Calvert died before he was able to go to Maryland. His oldest son Cecilius wanted to stay in England, so Cecilius sent his brother Leonard on the first voyage to the new colony. Leonard and 200 **colonists** sailed across the Atlantic Ocean and landed in Maryland on March 25, 1634. Some, but not all, of the settlers were Catholics. Leonard's father, Sir George Calvert, wanted people of different religions to make Maryland their home. When the settlers got to Maryland, they bought land for a town by trading axes and other tools with the local Native American tribes. The colonists called their town St. Mary's and made it the **capital** of their new colony.

Sir George Calvert was also called Lord Baltimore. Today, the city of Baltimore, Maryland, shares his name.

The journey to the colonies was hard, but people came hoping to find a better life. ▶

The First Settlers

Only 25 of Maryland's first 200 colonists were rich enough to pay for their trip to America themselves. They paid the way for other settlers who would become their servants. Calvert gave land to the rich colonists, who brought lots of people to Maryland. Each landowner was called a **lord of a manor**. Most lords were Catholics, and Calvert made sure that they were the ones to help him make the colony's laws. He didn't want Catholics to be **discriminated** against like they were in England.

Some of the colonists were skilled artisans, who helped make things all the colonists would need, like furniture, wagons, and farming tools.

Only a few lucky lords owned horses, which servants took care of.

Lords and Servants

Most of Maryland's first settlers were **bond servants**. After a lord of a manor paid for his servants' trip to America, the bond servants had to work for the lord for seven years. That time was called the servants' **indenture**. It was a very hard time for most bond servants. Their work was difficult, and their masters often beat them or wouldn't let them have enough to eat. When the indenture was over, servants could buy land and work for themselves. Unfortunately, many bond servants never became free. It cost a lot of money to start a farm, so many people had to work as servants for their whole lives.

Some criminals made money by capturing children, sneaking them aboard ships, and selling them as bond servants once they landed in the colonies.

Lords of manors could afford to keep many bond servants, who worked their land for them. ▶

Family Life in Maryland

Life in Colonial Maryland was hard in the 1600s. The colonists were still learning how to grow food in soil and weather that was very different from their home back in England. Colonists went hungry a lot of the time. Insects that caused sickness filled Maryland's swamps, and not many doctors had come to America yet. There was no one to care for the sick. In Maryland's early years, many adults died young. Almost every child in Colonial Maryland lost at least one parent. Parents often remarried if their husband or wife died, so children had lots of stepsisters and stepbrothers.

◀ *When their chores were done, children in Colonial Maryland liked to play outdoors with friends. They often had stepbrothers or stepsisters to play with, too.*

Working Life in Maryland

Like other southern colonies, Maryland's main business was farming. People who worked on their own small farms were called **yeoman farmers**. They fenced in their cornfields and other crops, but their pigs and cows roamed everywhere, even in the streets. Sometimes people had a hard time telling their pigs and cows apart from other people's. Whole families had to work hard every day. They did not have machines to help them farm, and only a few had horses or oxen. There were very few stores in Maryland. The colonists had to grow or make almost everything they needed.

For each male servant a lord brought to Maryland, he was given 100 acres of land. For each woman or child, he was given 50 acres.

Only a few farmers could buy horses. Most farmers had to do their work without them. ▶

Land, Tobacco, and Slaves

While yeoman farmers worked small farms in Maryland, lords had huge **plantations**. Bond servants worked the plantations until lords decided they wanted to use slaves. Unlike bond servants, slaves did not have to be set free after seven years. The Calverts had made slavery illegal in early Maryland because they thought it was wrong to own people. Even though it was illegal, in 1639, lords started to buy African slaves to work their plantations. Most lords grew tobacco, which they could sell for a lot of money.

It was illegal to grow tobacco in England. The king wanted the colonies to make money, so everyone had to buy tobacco grown in colonies like Maryland.

Some colonists used tobacco like it was money. They traded tobacco, grown on plantations like this one, for food, carts, or clothing.

The Plundering Time

Maryland's early colonists had a difficult time from 1644 to 1646. In England, people were fighting against each other in the English Civil War. One of the things they were fighting about was the unfair way different religions were treated there. Maryland's **governor**, Leonard Calvert, had to leave America and return to England. His brother, Cecilius needed help since the Catholics were having a lot of trouble because of the war. Many people, both Protestants and Catholics, fought for control of Maryland while Leonard Calvert was gone. There was no one in charge for two years. People acted like there were no laws, stealing from one another and fighting. These years were called "the **plundering time**."

Life was easier for the colonists when things finally calmed down after two years of confusion and fighting during "the plundering time." ▶

The Act of Toleration

Maryland was different from other colonies. The idea for Maryland came from Sir George Calvert's wish to start a colony that would welcome Catholics. In 1649, Maryland's lawmakers passed the **Act of Toleration**. That law made it possible for different kinds of Christians to live and work together. Christians who weren't Catholic could own land or hold public office. Many other colonies didn't **tolerate** different religious beliefs at all. Unfortunately, even with this law, some people in Maryland still weren't allowed to practice their religion. Jews, African slaves, and Native Americans weren't allowed to **worship** in their own way. For those times in history, Maryland's law showed a new way of thinking about religious freedom, but there was still a long way to go.

◀ *The Act of Toleration said that all Christians had the right to have their own religious beliefs.*

Living History

Today, Maryland's old capital, St. Mary's, is the home of the St. Mary's Living History Museum. Here you can visit **reconstructed** Colonial homes, inns, and workshops. You can sail into the past aboard the museum's full-scale model of the Maryland Dove, the boat that brought the first colonists to Maryland.

1632
King Charles I gives Sir George Calvert charter for a colony.

Leonard Calvert and 200 colonists settle in Maryland.
1634

1639
Slaves are brought to Maryland.

Protestants and Catholics fight to rule Maryland.
1646

1649
The Act of Toleration passed.

Maryland becomes a state.
1788

Glossary

Act of Toleration (ACT OF tah-luh-RAY-shun) A law passed in 1649 that said all Christians could practice their own religion in Maryland.

bond servants (BAHND SUR-vintz) People who have to work for someone for a certain number of years.

capital (KA-pih-tul) The place where the government for a certain area is located.

Catholics (KATH-liks) Christians who believe that the Pope is the head of the Church.

charter (CHAR-tur) An official paper giving someone permission to do something.

colonists (KAH-luh-nists) People who live in a colony.

colony (KAH-luh-nee) An area in a new land where a large group of people move, who are still ruled by the leaders and laws of their old country.

discriminated (dis-KRIH-mih-nay-tid) Treated unfairly.

governor (GUH-vuh-nur) An official that is put in charge of a colony by a king or queen.

indenture (in-DEN-chur) The length of time a bond servant has to work for a master.

lord of a manor (LORD OV UH MA-nur) Someone given a large area of land.

plantations (plan-TAY-shunz) Very large farms where crops like tobacco and cotton were grown. Many plantation owners used slaves to work these large farms.

plundering time (PLUHN-dur-ing TYM) The two years when Protestants and Catholics fought for who would rule Maryland.

Protestant (PRAH-tih-stint) A Christian who is not part of the Catholic religion.

reconstructed (REE-kun-struk-ted) A model built of an object or building from the past.

tolerate (TAH-luh-RAYT) To accept someone or something that is different.

worship (WER-ship) To pay great honor and respect to someone or something.

yeoman farmers (YO-min FAR-murz) A person who owns and farms a small area of land.

23

Index

Web Sites:

You can learn more about the colony of Maryland on the Internet. Check out this Web site: http://www.mdisfun.org/history/index.htm